THE HEART OF A HUSTLER

AN IMMIGRANT'S AMAZING JOURNEY
TO BUSINESS SUCCESS IN AMERICA

CHANTHAVY SINGVONGSA

The Heart of a Hustler

by Chanthavy Singvongsa

Copyright © 2021

All rights reserved. No part of this book may be produced, scanned, or transmitted in any form, digital, audio, or print, without the express written consent of the author.

ISBN: 978-0-578-32716-7

Publisher: Paul Jamison

www.chantsdailyhustle.com

CONTENTS

FOREWORD	1
1. COMING TO AMERICA	3
2. A BRIGHTER DAY	7
3. A MADDENING REVELATION	11
4. TROUBLED YEARS	15
5. DRINKING AND DRIVING	19
6. THE ROAD TO RECOVERY	23
7. LEARNING BY EXAMPLE	27
8. THE HEART OF A HUSTLER	31
9. FOR RICHER OR POORER, FOR BETTER OR WORSE	35
10. BEGINNING IN BUSINESS	39
11. BIRTH OF A HUSTLER	43
12. THE DAILY HUSTLE STORE	51
13. PROUD TO BE AN AMERICAN	57
14. CONSTANTLY IMPROVING	61
15. RESTRUCTURING THE BUSINESS AND FAMILY PRIORITIES	63
16. PASSING IT ON TO THE NEXT GENERATION	67

FOREWORD

You might ask yourself why a guy just approaching his 40 birthday would think he had enough life experiences to write a memoir. It might be a little nervy or even presumptuous, but after you read my story, I think you just might agree that it's been a wild and amazing journey.

I have gone from being six years old in war-torn Laos, to a refugee camp, and then on to the United States of America. I've had struggles with poverty, endured a chaotic and abusive family life, and traveled a rocky road through alcohol, drugs, and eventually to recovery.

My life began to change when the decision was made to no longer see myself as a victim. It takes a lot of courage to change. Once it's in motion nobody can stop it, only you. No doubt it is a big help when you have people come into your life at just the right time. But in the end, I still had to make the right choices and decisions to change. Thank you to my wife Amy, my Mother Souay Singvongsa, my patient and supportive in-laws, my mentors Roger and Carolyn Kahler, Marilyn Matejka, Tom Pribyl. Without each of you, my road would have been tougher.

When I first thought about writing a book, I knew it needed to add value to the reader. My hope is that by telling the story of coming from a troubled childhood, finding the inspiration to change, that others would believe it's possible in their life.

The summer of 2021, marked the 17th anniversary of my sobriety. In June of 2004, I finally said, "Enough with this!" I decided to quit drinking and using drugs. I had received treatment for 98 hours as an outpatient, not willingly, but at the mandate of the courts. In the beginning, I didn't think I had a drinking problem even though I had received three DWI citations in four years. There was always someone else to blame or some other excuse for my actions.

This is my story, the account of all that I've struggled through. Growing up I always wanted to be a part of something. I felt lost and never felt like I fit in. The alcohol use started in middle school and little did I know how drastically it would affect my life and what a dangerous path I would travel as a result.

Alcohol was used to feel better—to forget about anything that was bad in my life. Marijuana was smoked for the same reason. From that first drink in eighth grade, it was my go-to thing, all through the rest of middle and high school. I was drinking well before turning 21 and just about the time I could drink legally, I quit!.

Seventeen years later I've got a new life and am truly blessed. The "Guy Upstairs" has really helped me along the way and everybody that has been part of this process of staying clean and sober has made a big impact in my life. My wife and I now have two boys, two businesses, and a good life.

As I celebrate another sobriety day anniversary, I want to bring hope to those still struggling with addiction. There is help; there is hope. There is more to life when drinking and drugs are behind you. This story is my personal experience, not an attempt to bash anyone who drinks. However, if my story can help just one person who finds themselves in a similar situation to mine, then this effort will have been worth it. I hope this book helps.

Today I am a father and a husband. It feels so good to do these things that I once thought were impossible. I'm out of my shell. I'm still working on myself and always will be. To anybody who is struggling with the disease of drug addiction and alcoholism: there is a future. There is a better life!

1

COMING TO AMERICA

It is a frigid winter morning in Jackson, Minnesota. The alarm clock jars me awake at 12:30 a.m. Snow fell last night and my job is to get it plowed from driveways and parking lots in Jackson, Minnesota, and surrounding towns. The bed is warm and I dread getting up, but I must—I am an entrepreneur! It's just part of my business and what I signed up to do. People expect us to show up and do our job.

This is now a part of my Daily Hustle and a long journey from my humble beginnings.

My family—parents, two brothers, a sister, and I fled war-torn Laos in November of 1986. We were fortunate to find a way out of a country constantly embroiled in war and arrived at a refugee facility in the Philippines when I was almost six years old.

We stayed with a host family for about eight months and did not share a common language with them. Gestures and expressions were the only way to communicate. It was great fun playing with and enjoying being with other little kids. My mother's memories are not as carefree as my own and are not discussed in our family. However, as I got older, I came to understand her reasons. She likes to keep this period of her life in the past.

We were permitted into the United States because my dad had family here and because we were sponsored by a church in Omaha, Nebraska. I came here with my two brothers and one sister. Later, another sister was born in this country. My oldest sister remained in Laos so she could take care of our grandparents. She has never been to the United States and we have never been back there. We remain in touch and she is married with children of her own.

There was tremendous excitement to board an airplane that would take our family to the U.S. We were given hot dogs to eat on the plane—the first American food I ever ate. I remember those hot dogs clearly. They tasted delightful to six-year-old me.

Arriving in Omaha, we settled at my uncle's house but soon moved into government housing, a HUD house—our first home.

The adjustment was pretty easy for a kid. I accepted everything as okay because it was all I knew in this new and very different country. My brothers and I had ESL classes to learn the English language. I don't know how my brothers fared in their school experience, but a child of six learns and adjusts easily. Growing up I never had problems with bullying about being an immigrant because we were surrounded by other immigrants going through the same experience. Early childhood was just being a kid and having fun.

A little less than a year later, in May of 1988, we moved again to Austin, Minnesota, where my parents could find work and make some friends. They both went to school to get their High School GED. Mom took accounting classes. They worked a lot just to pay the bills and take care of our family.

Austin was the place where my mother and dad were working hard and trying to provide for us. Our household was very dysfunctional. Mother and Dad were always fighting about money and not having enough of it. Mom was trying to make the marriage work and provide a normal life for us kids.

Again, we were eligible for government housing. The HUD house we lived in was a two-bedroom ranch of about 800 square feet. It was a decent house but with five kids it was pretty crowded. The rent on the house was income-based.

In spite of meager circumstances, my brothers, sisters, and I were happy kids. We didn't know any different and the concept of being "poor" hadn't hit us yet. In the town of Austin, there were street concerts and dances for the community fairly often.

After those community events, there would be soda cans and beer cans on the street to be picked up and recycled helping us make some money. Mom would give each of us some garbage bags and we'd go around picking up cans. That was my very first taste of the "Hustle" and we were all happy to make a few extra dollars.

Mom would take us fishing and we spent that time as a family having fun, though my dad did not go with us. Austin has a lot of lakes and a river where we fished. Fishing has always been a part of our family's life. While we would be out fishing Mom would always pick some kind of blossoms growing on a tree and take them home to cook along with any fish we caught. She would always say to us kids that it was a certain kind of vegetable she would pick back in Laos but we kids knew better. All those things we did as a family are precious memories that I'll never forget. My mother kept us grounded and taught us how to "Hustle" early in life … more to come on that subject.

After a few years, another job opportunity for our parents brought our family to Jackson, Minnesota. This was in 1992, and I still live there today. I was ten years old at the time and in the fourth grade ... enjoying going to school and having plenty of good times.

Here in Jackson, we lived in another HUD house, same style, a small ranch. We thought it was great because we had a roof over our heads. As I grew older, I began to understand that we lived in housing provided by the government for those who needed help or could not afford to buy a house. We were looked down on as being a poor family.

My school in Jackson was very racially diverse at that time. We had Hispanics, some African-Americans, many Asians, yet the school was still mostly White. Jackson is a small town of about three thousand people occupying a little more than four square miles.

As I grew up, ninety percent of the Asians left Jackson, leaving only a few Asian families. They had moved to find work. As a close-knit community, if one Asian family finds out there are good jobs available somewhere else, others followed as they seemed to migrate together. Worthington, Minnesota, a town thirty miles from Jackson, had a meat-packing plant and that was one of the destinations. The other was Louisiana where many found work doing welding. Those jobs paid more than they could make in Jackson.

There used to be an Asian neighborhood here on First Street. Kind of our own community where everyone lived in rental housing. As a community, we played a lot of basketball and soccer there. We could walk to where everyone played as we lived nearby. It was a happy life as a small child but mixed with hard times. Though I was quiet and shy, as I grew older the constant arguing between my parents made me feel bad for my mother and wary of the man I called "Dad."

2

A BRIGHTER DAY

Our family situation became more and more chaotic as Dad changed from bullying just my mother to now bullying us boys. The bullying was mostly verbal, though he would always threaten us with a belt or a hammer. He had a short temper and often lashed out over small things. We were not allowed to discuss our dreams or what we wanted to do with our life. "Just keep your mouth shut," he would say. We were always walking on glass, including my mother. I felt sorry for her but there was nothing I could do for her as a child who was afraid.

Mom did what she could to get us out of the house into a calmer environment. We came home late one evening after attending an Awana event at church bringing leftover fruit home in a basket. Dad got upset with her because dinner had not been on the table when he got home from work. He began throwing the fruit around the kitchen in a rage. My mom should have been home, he said.

In another incident, my brother, Korak, and I were sitting down to eat and my dad began arguing with him about what time he was supposed to be home. I was afraid of him and It got to the point where the food did not taste good at all. I just wanted to leave the table. Korak decided to step up and say something rather than keeping quiet with our heads down as we usually did. Korak started voicing his thoughts and his own opinions. Next thing I know he was being beaten and threatened with a hammer. I was terrified and didn't know what to do except stay out of his way. That kind of thing happened in our household all the time. We were always scared as kids.

My mom did her best to raise us, but we were on our own a lot doing whatever we wanted to do. The constant money issue made us painfully aware of being poor. At the beginning of the school year, everybody would go out shopping while we wore hand-me-downs. I got my brother's old shoes and clothes and never had any of the nice things other kids had. It wore on all of us. There seemed to be no way out.

Poor to me is not having the ability to provide for the family and have the things we need and want—the things I grew up not having. Always, "We can't afford it." My brothers and I wanted to be in sports but could never pay for it. Mom couldn't pay even fifty dollars for the sign-up fee. It was always, "No, no, no—we can't." This was the root of problems and arguments in our house. I vowed to never let that happen in my future life. No fighting and yelling about money. That's why I do what I do today. I don't want my kids to grow up like that.

The concept of providing the best I can is what drives me today. At a deep level I know I don't want to be in a position of not having much—that I couldn't buy a decent pair of shoes or a decent shirt to wear. I don't want my kids to grow up in a dysfunctional house feeling less than they are.

There's never a "worst day" when you come from a place of darkness; there's always a brighter day to look forward to. The best thing that happened to me in fifth grade was getting to know Amy Mohns. Amy is now my beautiful wife.

Amy was in the sixth grade at middle school; I was in fifth, still in elementary school. Because we lived in such a small community, everybody knew one another. Though I was in a different school I ran into Amy from time to time. I was a shy kid, but nevertheless, when I wanted something I went after it. Once I knew what I wanted I was not shy about following through and I knew I wanted to get to know Amy. Dogged determination was something I was good at but did not normally use that ability until I was older.

Back then kids hung out a lot and weren't sitting at home in front of a screen. We would go to one another's houses and play. Amy ran with a crowd higher on the economic scale than my family, but I was attracted to her and pursued her. We got to know one another. I learned how to speak up and not quit. I knew I wanted to know this girl better and see what she was all about.

Her school often sponsored middle school dances. Fifth graders weren't allowed to attend but somehow, someway, Amy got me in there. I don't know how she managed to get me past the chaperones. I was not a big kid and Amy towered over me as we shuffled around slow-dancing, but we had a good time together that night.

After the dance, we spent a lot of time together just being with one another and getting to know each other. We "dated" this way through the rest of middle school. I felt Amy was someone who cared about me. It always goes back to the void of what I didn't have in childhood.

Then a family secret was revealed, and it changed the course of my young life.

3

A MADDENING REVELATION

Around this time I was in the eighth grade, a good friend of my mother let a dark family secret out. Unaware that we did not know this information, she mentioned that the man we knew as our dad was not our biological father. Resentment is too mild a word to describe my feelings upon learning this truth. Something broke inside of me and it would take years to start healing.

We confronted our mother with this revelation about our "so-called dad," but she refused to talk about it. All I know about my biological father is that he is still in Laos. We have never met him.

Why did she not feel she could tell us this? Why did she not stand up to my stepfather? I think it has a lot to do with her fear of him and fear of losing face to her friends. In the Asian community, everybody keeps family business to themselves. If there are problems you don't want to bring shame on the family, so her troubles were always brushed aside until she couldn't take it anymore.

To me, this was a lightbulb moment explaining the lifelong anger and bitterness my stepfather seemed to have for us boys. My two sisters are his blood and they are my half-sisters. I was sick at heart over the fact I did not know this man was not my blood but thought he was my father. I was angry and resentful toward Mom for not letting us kids know he was not our dad.

There was now a sudden switch in the way I was thinking and acting. My grades slipped to Ds and Fs. I started using drugs and alcohol thinking I was having fun. In reality, it was to hide everything taking place at home.

All that time this man was never our real father. He had never been good or kind to us. Maybe that was why he was so hard on us boys. I was not very kind to my mother all through high school and didn't care about hurting her with my behavior. She had lied and that was that.

My stepfather continued his bullying behavior. He hit my brother in the head with a clear intention of hurting him. He threatened us with a hammer or a bat but never hit us with those. He always put fear into us. How far would he go? The final time, though, there were punches thrown. We were not little boys anymore. That's when he realized we were not going to take his abuse. He was still verbally abusive but now he knew we would stand up for ourselves. Now the mistreatment has become more subtle.

As a teenager, I came home on a cold, winter Monday night at about nine o'clock. The door was locked, and I knocked to get in. My stepfather got up from his chair, saw that it was me, and went back to the chair to continue watching *Monday Night Football*. The rest of the family were already in their rooms staying out of his way.

Not being let into the house, I was forced to spend the night freezing in one of our unlocked cars. All night long he knew I was out there. I was boiling with anger the next morning when I saw him while he acted as if nothing had happened.

The constant fighting and chaos continued in our house. The fights were always about money, not having enough for anything. Then my parents began arguing about everything. My mother was reaching the end of her rope with his behavior. Eventually, the marriage ended in divorce and he moved to Minneapolis. I don't know if my mother ever got any support money from him for my two sisters. I was just glad he was out of her life and our lives.

4

TROUBLED YEARS

There was a time during middle school and while Amy was in high school where we split up for a few years. She was running with a different crowd and in fact, we didn't even talk to each other anymore. I started drinking and partying by the time I was in the eighth grade, not caring about school or anything else. All the kids were doing it and I joined right in.

By the time I was in high school, I very much wanted to get back to my relationship with Amy. I saw her at a party and began pursuing her. However, she said I wasn't her type anymore and that she was interested in another guy. The whole evening I kept pushing, talking and trying to connect but we didn't click that night.

Now both attending high school, we saw each other more and more and we would both be at those same parties. I wanted us to be together again. Prom came around and I asked her if she would go with me. If she didn't say yes, my plan was not going to work because I was only a sophomore and couldn't go without her! I was crushed when she said she didn't want anything to do with me. She was still interested in another guy. That other guy turned her down, so I kept pursuing, and we ended up going to prom together.

At our high school, the prom was a whole night event with everything taking place there at school. We got ready at her parents' house and went with another couple in the friend's car. We talked through the night and got that old connection back. After prom night we were together again, spending most of our time with one another after school and on weekends. When we were with friends there was always drinking and partying going on. All our friends participated and so did the two of us.

I used drugs and alcohol all through high school. I drank a lot. I smoked cigarettes, tried different drugs, and smoked pot. The one thing I always returned to was alcohol. Those were the only things that made me feel good and forget about all the bad things happening at home. Please don't see me as a victim—these were my own misguided choices—but I believe the chaos in my home was the reason I started down this road.

I drank. I worked. From the time I was sixteen, I worked at a *Best Western* motel restaurant in Jackson washing dishes. I went there after school and washed dishes until closing time. Always trying to advance, I worked my way up to being a cook. No handouts for me even though money was still the main issue at my house. At this time I did not realize or admit I had a drinking and drug problem. The only reason I was washing dishes was to have a few dollars to buy myself some nice things and support my habits.

It is no surprise that I started getting into trouble with the law. At age sixteen, I was out one night with a bunch of older guys when they decided it would be a good idea to steal a car and go for a joyride. Being high I simply went along with the crowd. I didn't know what the person who stole the vehicle intended to do with it, I was just along for the ride. We were picked up for Grand Theft Auto and legally I was just as guilty as anyone else. My minor status and the fact that I was not driving kept me from being prosecuted. I think I was released because of my mother who was named my "guardian."

I was released into my mother's custody and she is the one who came to pick me up that same night. Both she and my stepdad were angry and frustrated with me. I went to court where I pled guilty and was ordered to do community service. I wish I had could say it taught me a lesson, but that was not the case. I became even more rebellious, often saying to my stepdad, "You're not my dad. You can't tell me what to do!" There was constant arguing and friction between us. That same year, 1998, my mother filed for divorce and my stepfather moved out of our house.

There was so much of life I wanted to get busy experiencing. I felt I was wasting my time in school so I dropped out of high school a few months short of my graduation in my senior year and took a full-time factory job. Amy was already at a technical college in Faribault, Minnesota.

I decided my life was spiraling downward and I wanted full-time money as soon as possible. No time to waste sitting in a classroom. I told myself, "I just want to make money. I'm not going to college. I'm not going anywhere. Might as well quit school and get on with my life."

I was settling, I knew that, but I saw no real future. I was happy to get a job making $10 an hour. There was no vision of my potential; of what I could become. So I packed up my belongings and drove to Fairbult and lived with Amy in her apartment while she was going to college. I got a job at *Jennie-O* as a laborer working on the farm raising baby turkeys until they were ready to be moved to a finishing barn.

One day I noticed an ad in the local papers of an opportunity to make more money. It was an ad for selling Kirby Vacuums and offered substantially more income than what I was currently making at the Turkey store. The ad said they were only hiring a few people, so I quickly applied. Never in my life had I sold anything to someone. This would all be new to me.

At the hiring time, I was waiting in line with about 25 others for an interview. Thinking to myself this will be my big break to make big money just as they promised in their ad. It was my turn for the interview and trying my best to act as if I knew what I was going to say. After completing the interview, I went home hoping to be chosen. A week passed and I got the call. They hired me and this left me feeling very happy! I told Amy that we will not have to worry about money anymore and it's going to open up new doors.

I put in my two weeks notice at *Jennie-O* and was ready to start my new job. On the first day at the new job, we had orientation. They explained how we would get paid for this job. Dumb me! I had not realized I wouldn't get paid unless I sell a vacuum. I wasn't even guaranteed a paycheck and I had just quit my job that was providing weekly income. Not deterred, I remained determined.

For the next few weeks, I went knocking on doors with the owner of the company trying to sell some vacuums. I would watch him as he pitched and tried to sell but no luck. He would then give me CDs to take home and listen to about how to sell and become a good salesman. On my ride to work and back home, I would listen to the CD and then try the ideas I was learning on the clients, but I still couldn't sell even one vacuum. Finally, after one month of working there, we were having lunch at his shop and I needed a way out and to quit but was afraid to give him two weeks because If I gave him my two weeks notice that means two more weeks I wouldn't have a paycheck. I told him that I was going to go to the gas station and so I got up and left and never went back.

I got my job back with *Jennie-O* and worked my way up to be a Farm manager where they gave us a house on the farm to live in and take care of the turkeys there. Also noteworthy, I finally got my GED certification in January of 2009, almost ten years after I was supposed to graduate from high school.

5

DRINKING AND DRIVING

When I was eighteen I received my first DWI here in Jackson. Driving around town with friends, the police pulled me over for tinted windows that were too dark. We had to call a few people to find someone sober who could drive the car home. I didn't spend the night in jail, but I did lose my license for one year. It's definitely inconvenient to figure out how to get a ride every single day. Amy or one of my friends would drop me off at work. I was not allowed a work pass to drive to and from my job and resented having to ask for rides all the time. I had a drinking problem then and didn't want to admit it. I simply chalked it up to "bad luck" that I got pulled over.

I was resentful to the officer who stopped me and emphatically told him "no" when he asked if I had been drinking. He didn't believe me and proceeded to give me a hard time. I blamed him for hassling me. It was his fault. Nothing was ever my fault. I lived in total denial. After one year I received my driver's license back. Never did it occur to me to avoid a repeat of my behavior behind the wheel of a car, so I continued to drink and drive.

We lived in an apartment together up in Faribault where Amy was attending college. One night we were drinking at a friend's party in Jackson, and I was very drunk. I had a 2-door Honda stick shift—a two-seater. I drank so much and never should have attempted to drive, but I thought I could. Amy couldn't drive the stick shift and we had to get back up to Faribault because she had a job there as well as her classes. We had to get back that night.

Around midnight we were on the interstate heading north. I did not realize I was going 40 miles per hour in a 70 mph zone. Amy didn't notice because she was under the influence herself. Once again flashing blue lights and we were pulled over by a state patrolman and I got my second DWI. We had to leave the car at a gas station and call a friend for a ride to Faribault.

Losing my license for another year and incurring a fine as well as having to attend 12-step meetings convinced me that I didn't belong there. I wasn't crazy or addicted to alcohol! It did not register that this program was for me. This was my first experience with an addiction recovery program.

There were steps to follow in order to get my license back again. I had to go through the process, so I sat through those meetings and thought they had nothing to do with me. The first time I went to a meeting I walked in and saw a group of ten people. It was a strange feeling. They broke us up into two groups of five. Everybody was sharing their own feelings and experiences. I had been thinking I shouldn't be there, but when people started to share I thought, "They're talking about ME." I somehow felt they were picking on me when they were talking about themselves. But I still went home that night and drank. I didn't think I had a problem.

Amy was out of school now and I was depending on her to drive me around again. Lesson learned? Heck, no!

Amy and I moved out of our apartment and into her parents' basement. Once I moved out of my mother's house I did not want to go back. Amy's parents, Paul and Mary Mohns—I can't imagine what we put them through—what I have put them through. We lived with them for about a year in the basement of their house. In the meantime, I was working in Estherville Iowa in a meatpacking plant. Slaughtering pigs in what they called "the kill room." This is where the pigs were getting processed. I was making $8 an hour at the time and coming home with pig blood all over my face and clothing. I didn't care. I made money, that's all that mattered at the time. Here I was, a grown man who should be taking care of their daughter, and I was under house arrest, had an ankle bracelet, and was required to blow into a canister breathalyzer machine every so often. The only thing I was permitted to do was to go to work. Finally, the year was up, and the suspension was lifted on my driver's license.

I was twenty when I got my third DWI—not even old enough to legally drink. I was at a bowling alley with friends in Windom, Minnesota. There were about ten of us in three vehicles—mine and two others. We were bowling and I was taking shots. The older friends would buy the drink and I would sneak to drink it. Hide it until no one is looking. We drank and bowled until it was time to go to another house party.

I had DWI plates on my car by that time. Thinking I was so smart, I told the drivers of the other two cars to have one in front of me and one behind so I would be in the middle. We left for the party in Mountain Lake, only a few miles from Windom. Confident I would not get pulled over because the car behind me would be the logical target of any cop out there. Pretty quickly I saw flashing lights of a police car that pulled over the car behind me. I thought I had gotten away clean. My friend got to the side of the road but the next thing I knew the cop car pulled up right behind me. I think the officer was already waiting for us because he had spotted the DWI plates when we were still in the bowling alley parking lot.

He came up to me and asked if I had been drinking and I told him "no." "I smell alcohol on your breath," he said. "Well, I had a few but

I'm fine." He wasn't buying it and gave me my third DWI. I was in denial once again that I was drunk. Both friends left the scene, but the cop took me in that night, and I spent over a week in the Windom jail. This time I got a suspended license for another year because I had refused the sobriety test on the roadside. I refused because I had drugs in my system and had been smoking pot. I was on probation already and knew I was in real trouble.

It was cold in that cell. I felt like an animal in a cage. There was nothing fun about it. I was walked into the station, drunk, fingerprinted, and a mugshot taken. I was so intoxicated I didn't remember what had happened. I woke up in a little holding cell where they keep people in that condition. When I realized I was in jail, I had a feeling, for the first time, that something had to change in me. I thought, "Do I really have a drinking problem? What is this? Why do I keep getting myself into this situation?"

Appearing before a judge, he said I needed treatment. He made that determination because he could see the pattern that I was ignoring. The only time I was not in trouble was when my license was suspended and I wasn't allowed to drive. This was 2002. Back then they weren't as strict as they are now. The first offense was a slap on the wrist and losing your license. The second time, lose your license and go to the 12-step meetings. The third time, the decision is made to put the offender into outpatient treatment.

I had house arrest and outpatient treatment. We were living in Amy's parents' basement and had nothing left. No money. No drinking. Couldn't associate with my old friends or family members who all drank freely. I had no life but to go to work, come home, not see friends or family. Even though Amy was there and her parents, I was in my own miserable world wondering why things were this way and if I was ever going to have the life I wanted. Depression and loneliness set in.

6

THE ROAD TO RECOVERY

The third DWI required me to enter a 98-hour outpatient treatment center called *Road to Recovery*, followed by six months of aftercare at the *Ashley House*. I began to see my life change. Changes were essential if I was ever going to give up drinking. It was suggested I give up my crowd of partying friends. I did and never felt so alone. It was not something I wanted to do but I had to give them up. I knew it was the only way out of these destructive behaviors. I had to distance myself from my family and anyone who was part of my drinking habit to keep myself away from the temptation and focus on taking care of myself. Staying away from everything and everyone I knew was hard.

Amy stuck with me through all this. She came with me to treatments and meetings just to sit and listen. We would talk about it afterward. She did not think it had anything to do with her but was there to support me in my recovery. I have to think it helped her as well. We began to understand drinking was no longer to be a part of either of our lives and our life together. We were both trying to change, Amy and I distanced ourselves from all our old friends just to take care of ourselves.

Outpatient treatment was every week. We would sit around and talk about our problems. Additionally, I went to 12-step meetings three or four days a week. It was at one of these sessions that I was assigned Tom Trible as a sponsor to help me.

While in treatment, I was offered the opportunity to go into prisons to share my story with the inmates. I signed up to do that. The first time my sponsor and I went together, it was surprising how afraid I was. We had to go through the center of the police station, through the main portal, and walk through into a room to speak to these inmates. The scene held bad memories for me. That first time I said little, leaving it to my sponsor. Soon after I began going by myself and talking with these guys for about an hour. I did that for the next seven years.

Tom had been sober for five years. He is still my sponsor. If I ever have an issue or a desire to drink, he is the one I call. The beginning was the difficult part. Tom helped me through the twelve steps to get to the root of why I did these destructive things. Now I apply these steps to everything I do in life, anything I might struggle with. Early on I would call Tom three times a week to talk about what I was feeling and why I was feeling that way. I did not understand myself well at that time because I had never acknowledged those feelings. The loneliness I felt was overwhelming. I was floating through life without an anchor, a foundation. I felt like I didn't have a place.

At these meetings, I was open and honest in front of all these strangers. I found the help I needed to connect with the treatment counselor, Marilyn Matejka. She made the treatment program a safe place. I had trust issues—never felt I could trust people because of all I had experienced. For some reason in that outpatient center, I felt safe. I trusted Marilyn. We began talking and digging deep. At the same time, I was working through the twelve steps with Tom and those steps worked.

When I went to treatment, I got a taste of what life was all about, how good it could be. All I knew was one way of life and that was: Everything happens to me; I never have good luck. When I went into treatment life slowly changed. I started realizing, WOW, this isn't bad.

I'm no longer getting into trouble; I'm no longer getting arrested. I wasn't rich but I had a few dollars in the bank, not much but it was more than I ever had before.

I always thought I was born unlucky. Now I discovered that "luck" takes work and commitment. When I stopped using alcohol and drugs people showed up in my life that I normally would not have surrounded myself with. Solid, caring people who showed me the way to a better life.

I was on the road to recovery.

7

LEARNING BY EXAMPLE

I met Roger and Carolyn Kahler at a picnic where my treatment group gathered in the back of the *Ashley House* in 2004. They were there to lend some support to Marilyn, my counselor, who was a friend of theirs. For some reason, they took an interest in me. I never knew why—maybe Marilyn said something to them about me. Sometime later, Marilyn's father passed away and I went to the funeral. That is when I met up with Roger and Carolyn again.

Roger ran a business on his farm called *Kahler's Custom Iron*, making iron railings and other items. He asked me if I was interested in working with him part-time at his shop. I was not sure if I could manage that, but I had a big credit card debt to pay off, so I agreed. I started work at 5:30 a.m. at the factory and got off around 4:30 and then went out to Roger's place to help him at his shop every day. I worked there until 9 or 9:30. I worked for Roger and Carolyn for the next four years.

Amy was home by herself and we were trying to get our life together. There would not be another woman in the world who would put up with all that I put her through. Working with Roger was like a retreat for me to get away from everything in my regular life. The job was creative and did not feel like work to me. I grew to appreciate these people so much. They did not have to do what they did for me while

I was out there working with them. I was learning by their example. They taught me how to be a son, a husband, and though parenthood was still a few years away, they taught me how to be a dad as well.

I was learning by their example. My family was so dysfunctional—all drama. There was no kindness. When I went to this couple's house, they were in their late 50s at the time, it felt safe to me. Growing up I always felt like someone was going to harm me or take advantage of me. I trusted Roger and Carolyn and felt I could share my thoughts, my dreams, my vision of what I wanted my life to be like and nobody would get upset with me. They encouraged me to pursue my dreams.

Roger understood me and knew I was uncomfortable in my own skin, afraid to talk to people and to make decisions. I was always scared because I had always been told what to do by others. Roger was the opposite. He would draw me out of my shell in creative ways sending me to interact with customers.

One time he made a candle stand for a church. He said to me, "Chant, could you deliver this? Ask for so-and-so and tell him you are delivering the piece he ordered." I was scared but Roger gave me the responsibility of doing those uncomfortable things I did not want to do. I learned how to be more at ease around people I did not know, how to talk to people, and not to be so afraid.

Working on the farm, there were times when we harvested apples. I was driving out to their farm to help pick apples and I was thinking, "I'm picking apples and he's paying me MONEY?" I did not understand this. Why would someone pay me to pick apples, or dig potatoes, or plant things? It didn't feel like work to me. I liked doing those things. Everything we did was—WOW, I am enjoying this!

During those harvest times, we would go in for a coffee and cookie break. We sat around the table and Roger and Carolyn would pray before we ate our snack. We would talk. I didn't understand why they cared about me and my life. Growing up I never had that. Again, I don't want to play the victim, but the reality was I wasn't used to such caring kindness.

I grew quite a bit as a person by working with the Kahler's. They allowed me to dream and see who I wanted to be and what I wanted to do. They encouraged me to stretch as a person. I hadn't decided exactly what I wanted to do in life, but I realized, working with Carolyn in her garden, that I loved getting my hands dirty. She was an avid gardener who took care of numerous plants and flowers—annuals and perennials. We would plant and prune and split hostas. She offered me plants to take home to put around the house that Amy and I had just purchased. I couldn't say no, so I learned something about gardening and plants.

The Kahler's came into my life with perfect timing. I began making a commitment to turning my life around and now had a passion for gardening and digging in the dirt. At that time, I had no thoughts of getting into the lawn care and landscaping business. I was just out at the farm helping Carolyn. I loved working with Roger in the metal shop but that was not my passion.

It was hard to tell Roger I was leaving him because I didn't want to disappoint him. One day I told him about wanting to start my own lawn care and landscaping business. He gave me his full encouragement to go ahead and do it and he would help me all he could. He wasn't mad or upset. I knew I needed to quit working with Roger and asked him if that was okay. It is funny to me now, I was a grown man, but still thought I had to ask permission to pursue my own path. Roger and Carolyn had the opposite idea. They would tell me, "This is your life and you make the decisions that are right for you."

8

THE HEART OF A HUSTLER

Amy and I bought our house in 2007 and in order to take care of the yard I needed to purchase a lawnmower. Money was very tight then, but my credit score was finally decent. I went to Sears and bought a Craftsman push mower with a small bagging system in the back of the mower. The price was $250, and I had no idea where that money for payments would come from, but, like always, I knew I could figure it out.

I went knocking on about twenty doors around my neighborhood. Out of those twenty, one man, Allen Krebs, who lived a block west of us, hired me for a weekly mowing of his lawn. Every Saturday I would take care of his yard for $30. Mr. Krebs was the first sale I ever made. At that point, I didn't realize lawn care would or could turn into a business. I just knew I needed the extra cash to pay for my lawnmower.

Now my mind was working, "I knocked on twenty doors. Maybe if I knock on twenty more doors, I'll get another job—and then another… If I get ten more jobs that's $300 a week." I was only bringing in $350-400 bucks a week from my factory job. If I can get enough people to say yes, I can make as much as the factory pays me for my full-time job and turn it into a business. The work was more enjoyable to me and I loved working outside.

That first "yes" from Mr. Krebs planted that seed and my thinking shifted from that moment. "Okay, there is something here." I was offering lawn mowing services for less money than others and only wanted to get some consistent cash. I did not think about the end of the lawn mowing season when there is no grass growing or beyond the next three months of the growing season or I never would have taken that first step. I told myself I needed to make X-amount of dollars and I'll figure out the rest. In the meantime, I'm going to keep doing the lawn cutting and add services as they come up.

The clientele built up and I was happy to get a few dollars here and there. It began to add up to more than I was making at the factory. I bought my first truck and it became a tool to increase business. All I had then was that truck, the small walk-behind mower, a wheelbarrow, and a shovel. All I saw ahead was an opportunity.

Customers would ask if I could do landscaping and I would tell them yes, even though I didn't know anything about it. Again, I knew I could figure it out. YouTube was not in existence then and so I bought books on landscaping and how to start a landscaping business. There were books and audiobooks on plant identification and other things related to the business. I had never read books in my life but reading those fed my fire to build up this business. When I do things in my life it becomes obsessive. That's why I do the things I do today. In those early days, my customers paid for me to learn.

My experience with Carolyn helped too. I learned the names of all the plants she gave me to take home and how to care for them. My pay at the factory was $13 an hour, and I figured my first landscaping jobs were paying $15. Now I'm thinking, wow, I'm making two dollars an hour more. That was exciting until I realized I wasn't figuring in insurance, taxes, gas, or time to pick up materials and get to the job site. I was learning and making mistakes along the way.

By 2009, I had enough accounts to leave the factory job and do lawn mowing full time. Looking for ways to advance my business was a priority. When a customer asked me if we could do brick pavers, I said yes. I had no idea how, but I told him I could. That's when I hired an experienced worker named Kevin who had done landscaping for many years. Even though I didn't know landscaping or pavers, he did. He taught me and helped me with projects. I learned a lot from Kevin and slowly took on small jobs I knew I could handle. The business grew as my skills improved. If anybody asked me if I could do something, I would always say yes and figure it out.

People look at me as an expert. I wasn't lying to them because I knew I could figure it out and accomplish the job. If I told them I had never done that before, they would hire someone else. So, I always say yes first and figure it out second.

I was beginning to understand that my passion was owning and growing a business! Being able to create something and build on it, to offer a service to somebody, help them, while making a living for me and my family. I love building a business from the ground up, investing my time, and enjoying the process. I am good at putting systems in place, building a team, and making it work. The Heart of a Hustler was picking up momentum and every hobby I pursued became a business I would try to monetize.

9

FOR RICHER OR POORER, FOR BETTER OR WORSE

June 14, 2004, was the last time I took a drink or used drugs. I graduated from my 98-session long treatment program but would continue to attend 12-step meetings for a while. I never felt abandoned and am grateful for all the mentors and friends who were there to help me through any difficult patches. Amy stuck with me through it all. She was the first thing in my life I ever committed to. Amy and her family were there for the graduation from treatment. I asked her father's permission to marry Amy that night. I'm sure he had reservations. I don't know what they saw in me or thought of me. Up until then, I was always in trouble.

We were married on August 25, 2005, in Jackson at a place called Peace Park, a little park with a cascading waterfall. We took our vows standing on the rocks on top of the waterfall. There were about sixty people at our wedding reception at a local country club. It was hard for us because we were trying to stop drinking and partying. We made the decision not to serve any liquor at the reception. The bar was there if anyone wanted a drink, but they had to pay for it. We told everyone ahead of time, "If you want to be there, you can be there for us, but here's what we are going to do."

We celebrated with our family and people who are most important in our lives and left the reception around 10 p.m., long before most newlyweds leave their own party. We knew once everybody started drinking, we should get out of there. Honestly, it was hard as some of our old friends and family members were drinking. My sponsor always told me, "If you ever feel the situation doesn't feel right, pick yourself up and leave." At our own wedding, we did that even as the party was just getting started.

The next day we left for our honeymoon. We were excited to get away, just the two of us. We drove up to Duluth, Minnesota. It was the kind of trip we had never done together. We stayed near Lake Superior surrounded by the spectacular natural beauty of the place. We hiked and spent time in nature, staying in a wonderful hotel overlooking the lake. It was a good time of life—just trying to figure everything out between us. We were determined to do this together—change our course and face the next challenge.

When I was drinking, even though I had a job, I was taking out personal loans. All I did with that money was buy booze and nice clothes. I was close to $40,000 in debt. Amy was aware of this when we married.

When I got into treatment and started working on myself, it was time to make amends. That is one of the twelve steps. You have to make amends not only to people you've hurt or wronged but the creditors and banks you are indebted to. It was tough, but I was able to pay down those debts and begin cleaning up my credit while I was still in treatment.

I walked into my bank to ask for help. It was there I started working with Jeff Davis—another one of those people who showed up in my life when I needed him. He asked me, "What can you afford as a monthly payment to pay down these debts?" We started out with a $5,000 loan at a much lower interest rate than my credit cards. I committed to $400 a month. Jeff would take that loan money and pay some of those credit cards down. After I got that paid off, I took out another bank loan to continue to pay the credit card companies. If I had stuck with those higher interest rates, I never would have paid those off.

The debt was already in collection service. That's where the bank could help. Jeff knew I was getting sober and wanted to clean up my life and he was willing to work with me. Slowly, I tightened my belt. I worked at the factory; I worked out at Roger's—doing all these things for extra money to pay off those debts and buy a house. It took almost three years to pay all that off.

By 2007, we were finally able to take out a $60,000 mortgage for our house. A home of our own is important to us. Our house is small but big enough. There is room for our kids and now we have a finished basement and another bedroom upstairs. As long as we have a roof over our heads, we'll put our money back into our business. We are still young. Once we get older, if the business income allows us to buy a different house, that would be great.

On moving day, the people there to help us were people who had been in recovery with us. We had made those new friends and cut the old ones loose. We now had a bit of a social circle.

10

BEGINNING IN BUSINESS

In 2009, I quit the factory job and started *Singvongsa Landscaping Company*. Amy had worked at the same factory and she had already left that job to take an opportunity presented to her by her mother. Her mom wanted to retire from a daycare business she ran out of her home and Amy was able to transition that over to our house. Our first son, Ashton, was born on April 15, 2009, and she was able to be home with him. We converted our full basement into a daycare facility for up to ten children.

The only thing I did then was basic lawn care during the mowing season. I made just the same as when I was at the factory, but I had no benefits. We just had enough to pay our bills.

Jackson's only laundromat came up for sale and it was on a prime piece of property. I told Amy we should buy the laundromat and she laughed at me, "How are we going to afford that? We don't have any extra money." "I don't know but I'll figure it out."

I did my due diligence. Working with Roger I learned a little bit about running a business. He had been open and helpful in teaching me how he ran his custom metal business. I went to the realtor and asked about the property. I knew to ask for three years' worth of profit and loss statements. I looked at the numbers and they looked okay, but the asking price was much higher than what the business produced.

Even though It seemed like it wouldn't work, I didn't want to give up.

A couple of months later it was still bugging me—there had to be a way to make this work and I knew I wanted that property. My landscaping business was growing, and I was operating it out of our house, with the kids in daycare at our house every day, it was just getting impossible. There was no room. We were still living paycheck to paycheck. This laundromat business was located in a 25 x 30-foot shed that I really wanted along with the property. I didn't really care about the laundromat, but the property would be great for the growth of my business.

I went to see Jeff Davis at the bank. He had been working with me for some time getting my credit back on track and he knew my situation—what I was doing—my credit history. I told him I wanted to buy the laundromat and what they were asking for it—about $225,000. He wanted to know what the numbers looked like. I showed him the financials and he agreed it just did not work at that price.

Jeff had known me from the time my credit was a disaster and had worked with me for four years to clean it up. He knew I was a hustler, a hard worker, and would not let him, or the bank, down. I had credit built up when we bought the house we were living in. I wanted my next financial move to be the purchase of the laundromat.

Jeff told me there were a few ways this might work. Three ways of negotiating. He listed them and explained to me how these options could go if they really wanted to sell. We had to negotiate the price down so the income was enough to pay the mortgage and other bills.

Our offer to the seller was $150,000 and I had to come up with 20% down, or $30,000. At the time we only had a few hundred dollars in the bank and were living week-to-week. How could this possibly work? I went home to talk it over with Amy and she was still not sure this was the right thing to do. We had a baby, no extra money, and no cushion for emergencies.

A few days passed and I went back to the bank. I asked Jeff if anyone else could help me with that 20% down, a small business loan, or some other type of loan, to make this all happen. He connected me with *Southwest Minnesota Foundation*, an organization for small business start-ups in the southwest Minnesota area. The interest rate was higher, but I knew I wanted this opportunity to take on this laundromat and make it work. I knew I had to start somewhere and that being in business for myself was the only way to go.

When I started landscaping and mowing, I took all the 401K monies I had built up and invested it into the new business, buying some equipment, and helping pay the bills while I built the business. I am a risk-taker, knowing when I jump in, I will figure out a way to make it pay.

I was all in.

11

BIRTH OF A HUSTLER

We closed on the purchase of the laundromat and the property on December 23, 2010. It was now ours. An 80 x 90-foot lot and a 25 x 30-foot shed to house my landscaping operation. And a new business to learn and run.

My time in the laundromat business was definitely a strange time for me. I was staying sober and trying to figure out what my life was going to be. What am I doing? What was my purpose? I have no friends now. Nobody was around except Amy and our toddler son, Ashton. The only people I could count on were Roger Kahler, who helped advise me with my business and my life, and Tom Prible, my sponsor through the 12-steps and beyond. Tom had his own plumbing business and he helped me stay clean and sober, drug and alcohol-free.

Every morning I would wake up, open the laundromat, go about my landscaping jobs, come home at night and close the place up. We were open every day, including holidays. The responsibility was constant, and it was not much fun. After a year there was not a lot of profit to show —enough income to pay the bills and that's about it. The town was not growing and so the income did not grow, but the cost of doing business did. We never took any money home from the business. Money that we made from the laundromat went back into improving the building, electricity, maintenance, and mortgage.

We wanted to find a catchy name for the business and a logo that would pop. We named it Wishy-Washy Laundry and created a logo that was blue with bubbles and a sign that was bright yellow and blue that you couldn't miss. I spent time trying to figure this out. Why was I doing this? I told myself it was a start—an opportunity to own a business.

Our son, Cole, was born in March of 2013, and Amy and I wanted to make it a family business. We would bring Ashton and Cole in to help sweep up and wipe down the machines, giving them a sense of family working together. Slowly I was trying to improve it but no matter what I did, it did not give me a passion for the business. Though it was the only laundromat in town, the customer base was stagnant and not growing. The thought had not occurred to me yet that one day I would sell all that equipment, get out of the business and go in a completely different direction.

Sometimes you have to start where you can, explore other options, and move on. By the time I moved my landscaping business to the new site, I had a few residential snow plowing accounts. We bought our first dump truck, a 3500 Chevy with a plow, and it opened the door to taking on bigger accounts. In Minnesota, snow plowing in most years can be an enormous boost in income. The extreme change of seasons puts the earth to sleep but awakens the hustle in me.

Here in our home state, we can feel the snow coming in with a drop in temperature and the increasing moisture in the air. At the same time, we must rely on the prediction on the weather app. It is not always accurate. Once in a while, our team goes to bed expecting to go to work past midnight and we end up with a slight dusting of snow after a 4-6 inch prediction. We meet at the shop at about 1 a.m. and discuss our schedule and our routes. Everybody gets into trucks and we head out to our locations.

I have a team of up to eight people, equipment operators, and shovelers. The shovelers will clean up the sidewalks and entrances. Equipment operators and truck operators take care of the big parking lots. By now it is 2 a.m. and the streets are quiet. There is a feeling that the whole town is just for us so we can play in the snow—to do what we do. The only sounds shattering the quiet are the backup alarm of the skid loader and the plow hitting and scraping the pavement.

It is a different feeling when we are out at that time of the morning. The world is asleep, the snow falls softly, quietly muffling every other sound. We are alone in an alien world of frigid stillness. The job takes ten or eleven hours to complete, depending on the amount of snowfall. The sun comes up while we are out and our bodies tell us we are ready for rest, but we can't do that right away. We push through as long as it takes. The world is coming alive, but we are not. The team is ready for bed. I spent the day trying to get my body back on schedule. There is other work to be done. Snow removal is only part of my day. Sleep comes later.

At our new worksite, there was office space on the other side of the building. At first, I rented it out to generate some cash flow. That tenant left and I started a phone repair business in that space in 2014. My phone was always getting damaged, and it was costing me money to have it repaired. Either I would drop it in the snow, drop a cement block on it, or plow over it. That forced me to learn how to repair cell phones. I took my phone to my brother, Phon, and we ordered the parts. I watched him fix the phone in his garage. It occurred to me that other people must have this same problem and need to have their phones repaired. My brother, Korak, could fix phones as well and I told him I wanted to start a side business. He thought I was crazy but a month or so later I started *I-Mobile Solutions Phone Repair*. Now we had the laundromat, the landscaping and snow plowing, the phone repair, and Amy was still providing daycare out of our home.

After a while, I had to let the phone business go. I came to the realization that I just couldn't do it all. I'll try just about anything legal and moral. Shortly before I began my path of sobriety, my brother Korak and I went into the mobile DJ business for about a year. I was into music back then and we thought it would be fun to build up that venture. We played at weddings and rented out a hall around our area, circulating flyers promoting weekend dances. People would come from all around the area to dance and party. It did not take me long to figure out this was not the best surroundings for a guy trying to stay sober. It got to the point where I was not drinking and was certainly no longer feeling comfortable in that environment.

Tom Prible, my sponsor, advised me on what to do and let me know that when I got that uncomfortable feeling, that I was either going to drink or had to get myself out of that situation. I spoke to him about the DJ venture, and he suggested two things I could do—either quit the DJ enterprise or cut way down on the operation. People in 12-step programs are often resistant or hesitant when someone "tells" them what to do. It should come as more of a suggestion, and be left up to the individual to make that decision. I did not want anyone either enabling me or nagging me. Tom was there to help me make the right decision. Even though there was a decent amount of money in it, I told my brother I was out. We sold off the equipment and I quit the DJ business.

Growing up, my mom never took pictures of us kids. We have very few photos of when we were little. When my son, Ashton, was born in 2009, I started a photography business. Amy and I wanted to take special pictures of our son. We hired a lady here in town and she did amazing work. It cost a few hundred dollars, but I wanted my children to have nice pictures of their childhood to look back on. We couldn't keep having ex[ensive professional photos taken, so I went to Walmart and bought a good Canon camera. I justified the expense knowing once I had the camera paid for, I could take as many pictures as I wanted of our family and they would be good ones.

I learned how to use and shoot manually with that camera—all about the F-stops and apertures and the multiple things a quality camera can do. I purchased more lenses. An idea germinated, "I can turn this into a business and have that camera pay for itself." That $600 camera made me a couple of thousand in revenue and I became obsessed with photography. I loved operating a camera.

I took pictures of my boys all the time. We went out in the fall and other seasons and I shot dozens of photos. They look just as good as the ones the professional photographer took of our firstborn as an infant. That's when the photography business was started. My first session was with a newborn. One of our friends asked me to take pictures of their baby. I charged about $50 for the session. It should have been more but they were friends and I was new at it.

The word spread and I booked sessions with entire families, then senior pictures for the high school. I even improved enough to be hired as a wedding photographer. Now doing weddings, I started doing videography. It became a good side hustle. Sessions were scheduled around my lawn care business.

I was unknowingly building up a skillset I'd use in the near future. In 2014, bored and restless with my businesses, I got on social media and discovered YouTube, and began sharing my day-to-day life. I recorded my day from the start in the laundromat, going out to mow lawns and water the plants in downtown Jackson where I had a contract to perform this service. If I did something, I recorded it and put it out there. I started to feel excited again. That this was what I was looking for.

It takes work to post videos—time to edit, time to shoot—not to mention all the camera gear that goes into making content. It takes a lot to be transparent and to share your life with the world. I would not change it one bit hoping to inspire and motivate even one person to change their life and let them know I didn't come from a background full of unicorns and rainbows.

For two years I put out a video every day, doing the day's editing in the evening. The only views I got were from people who knew me. I did not care. I was enjoying it, having fun, and documenting my journey. I have realized the hustle is in my blood and I have a passion for what I am learning about entrepreneurship along the way. On YouTube, I was connecting with over 26,000 subscribers and showing them what it takes to start from nothing, build a successful business and positively influence others.

When I started on YouTube I had my full name on the channel making it difficult for people to search and find it. And it certainly was not catchy. In 2016 I renamed the channel. I've always called myself Chant, a short version of my first name, so people could remember it. I was sharing my life on YouTube, vlogging every day, and documenting my life. I was not interested in making money with this, I just wanted to document my life. All I saw was the hustle—I'd wake up and record myself going down to the shop and opening up. Doing the things I do each day, I called it Chant's Daily Hustle. Then I started putting that on my company trucks.

In the beginning, I had some bad feedback about using the word "hustle." People thought it was a bad thing—like a scam or something—but there is another definition. Going out to bust your butt to make stuff. I knew where I wanted to take this and now it has become my brand.

Followers began to pick up in numbers. People became interested in what I was doing. Before long, they began to ask for "merch." They wanted hats and shirts with The *Daily Hustle* logo.

I found a local business to make custom hats for me to sell on YouTube. The quality was not what I wanted to be selling and I never knew if my order would get to me on time. I was not in control of production. It wasn't fast enough—nothing is ever fast enough for me. Another idea was born. I began to wonder, why is it hard for me to shut my thoughts off on business ideas? A lot of entrepreneurs go through this—is it just our nature? Sometimes we are hard on ourselves for where we think we should be, but I try to take a moment to reflect on what I've built and accomplished and know that what I have now would have been thought impossible in my past life.

12

THE DAILY HUSTLE STORE

In the winter of 2018, the snow removal business was slow. There was no money coming in and plenty going out to keep up with bills and payments. At the time Amy was still running the daycare business out of our home, caring for about ten kids each weekday.

I knew nothing about embroidery machinery—all I knew was we needed a machine to produce hats to meet customer demands. After some research, we bought a single head embroidery machine for $12,000. When it came in, we set it up in the space where I had been fixing phones.

I wanted to make hats with my brand for the *Green Industry Exposition* that is held every year in Louisville, Kentucky. My company was sponsored by a few brands and I was producing hats with their logos as well. *Bobcat Mowers* and *Jobber* were two of our clients. Up till now, these were items we had been ordering from the local company that did not meet my quality standards.

I needed to learn how to use this new piece of equipment ASAP. I drove about an hour and a half to Sioux Falls, South Dakota, to a mall where there was a store called *Lids*. *Lids* sells hats and customizes them to order right on the premises. I watched as the operator created a custom hat on their machines which was similar, but not exactly the same as my new one. I spent close to $60 on a gray hat and wanted the operator to customize it with my logo, "#Hustle." I watched the woman at the store and asked her if I could record what she was doing. She agreed. I recorded everything she did from setting up the machine to the completed product. When I got home with the hat and watched the recording, carefully setting up my machine.

It was a rocky start, and I had many questions. I called *Lids* that same day to speak with the machine operator there and see if I could pay her to come to teach me. At first, she agreed, but then she bailed on me. I had to find another source of information. In the end, I learned to operate my machine from *YouTube*. I think there is a tutorial for just about anything you want to learn there.

The owner of the embroidery business in downtown Jackson asked if I would be interested in buying her business. That company had been my source for the hats I had been selling. I was not ready to buy another business, especially in those slow months that winter, but I looked at her books and numbers. It still made no sense to buy her out, but I believed I could take it from where it was to where it is now.

We got creative. We negotiated a deal on what the business was worth, what I would pay for it, and what the owner would accept. She was asking $25,000 for the total business. I would put down $1,000, make payments with interest for two years, and have a balloon payment of $12,000 at the end of two years. The offer was accepted. We wanted to move this process quickly and turn over the keys fast.

The keys were handed over on January 1, 2019, and we were off to start our new venture. When two parties want to make something happen, you can find a way. I took over that business and kept their one employee on my payroll. I knew little about the operation and was depending on that experienced person to teach me what she knew. A week later she walked out because she was upset by the big change in ownership and different management style. In the middle of the day, she left and taped the key to the door. I came back to find the door locked and the key taped in plain sight. At that moment I realized she was not coming back. Now I was left to do everything by myself.

Amy was still doing daycare. I then was forced again to make some quick decisions. I was by myself trying to run an embroidery business and our snow removal and landscaping business. We were getting orders online from people that have been watching me on *YouTube*. Those orders kept us afloat. Amy agreed to quit her daycare business and come help me with the Embroidery business. Just like that, she gave her notice to the daycare parents that she was quitting. While I was waiting for Amy to come on board full-time with me I closed down the retail Embroidery store to catch up on the online orders and restructure the shop and give it a fresh look.

Amy and I are both new to this business. We were both struggling and getting frustrated at one another. We had orders to get out and obviously she had Mother duties as well, all while trying to be the best wife supporting me. We were both feeling the pressure. There were moments in the back room of the shop where we would take lunch breaks and not speak to each other. We both wanted to give up. We questioned our marriage, we questioned if we were doing the right thing but like everything in life that Amy and I have gone through we knew all it takes is communicating with one another. Sharing our feelings and thoughts of how we both felt then let's figure out the solution and that's what we did. It was then we hired our first employee to help with the business to take some pressure off of Amy.

In less than 4 months we outgrew the Downtown shop and I was looking to build or buy a building to expand our business but no buildings were on the market. One night closing up the laundromat as I was cleaning and looking around at the laundromat I thought to myself we have the perfect building and location to grow our embroidery business and the *Daily Hustle* brand. It was right in front of my face.

After the laundry equipment was sold, we started the space renovations within a month to house the new operation. I kept photos of different stores that I admired. Amy and I went to T*he Mall of America* and took pictures of various store setups to get ideas of what we wanted our space to look like. I started to build on those ideas. We got the contractors lined up and told them to get it done as soon as possible. I paid extra for that, but I didn't want it to take forever. They came in, and in a month it was all remodeled. We could start moving the embroidery equipment in and filling up the space.

I knew I wanted black and white décor, which was our brand color. I knew I could build some of the furniture myself, but I wanted it to look clean and modern. I am not skilled at building so I hired help and bought ready-made furnishings so they would look clean, fresh, and professional from the beginning.

Everything worthwhile in business and in life takes a little work and we are truly blessed to have a great team. When I started my operation, customers would complain about how we had changed the price structure and other things they did not like. The locals were still not happy with us for closing the only laundromat in town. As a business person, I had to do what was right to keep us afloat. The previous owner seemed to do a lot of things for free. I recognized that was not the way to make money and prices had to change.

By this time, I had quite a few followers on social media—21,000+ on *YouTube*, 2-4,000 on *Facebook*, 10,000 on *Instagram*. These were mostly contractors who had been watching my content. When I announced via social media that I was buying the embroidery business, they were eager to support the venture. We had no systems in place to take orders and 90% of our business was coming in online. The rest were local customers who had been the customers of the previous owner. With Amy's help, we scrambled to get an organization in place so we could create products and fulfill our orders. It was a busy time but a stimulating rush to get up in the morning and get going. I love when a business is in its infancy and everything has to be figured out.

I have found that business creation and development is my passion. When you get excited and can't wait to wake up to do what you do, you have found your calling. One day this will be a $1,000,000 company. It can be done no matter how small a town you are from as long as you have the right plan and team and are willing to grow and change. When there is a problem, you find a way to fix it. Don't wait for anyone or anything to come fix it for you. Many start-up business owners are not patient enough to see the result of putting in the work. They want all their problems to disappear. Action will carry you through tough times. Never discount what your knowledge and experience are worth and follow your instincts.

13

PROUD TO BE AN AMERICAN

I believe in America as the land of opportunity and I am, in fact, a living embodiment of that belief. When I was 23 years old, I was not even considering going through the process of becoming a citizen. The news media were expressing the idea that, if Donald Trump was elected, he was planning to deport anybody who was not a citizen. Of course, that was only my interpretation of what I was hearing. I was concerned even though I had not done anything wrong. I was a Legal Alien and carried a Green Card. Amy and I had kids by then and I didn't want to be deported, so I looked into the citizenship process.

I paid almost $700, which I did not have to spare at that time, to start on the path of becoming a citizen. There was a waiting period to see if the application would be approved. A few months later, I heard back from the government and went to take a test. I drove for about an hour and a half up to Minneapolis and entered a government building with security at the entrance. They checked for weapons and I went through a metal detector.

There were all races and many languages represented in the people waiting to take their test. I was prepared—it was like a social studies test to me—and I took the test. The results were not given right away to know if I had passed or not. I waited a few more months and received a letter saying I had passed. The next step was a face-to-face interview.

I made an appointment to do that.

Before the interview, I had to go to every county or court where I had gotten into trouble in my past to get a record that had to be stamped and verified at the courthouse. I drove around to the different towns where I had police trouble, going to every court to get all those documents. I was afraid I was going to forget something. Fortunately, all the records were verified, and I could then go to my interview.

When I arrived for the interview, it was in a small room with one man asking me questions. It was intimidating and felt like an interrogation—not welcoming at all. It was as though he was suspicious of me and wanted to trip me up. I thought it might be because I had been in so much trouble when I was younger. I had a police record. I was afraid I might not be accepted as a citizen.

I knew I could not leave anything out if I wanted the chance to be a citizen. We were in that small room and he kept asking more and more questions. I felt like he was trying to trigger me into getting upset about it—a test to see if I could control myself. By that time in my life, I had stopped blaming everyone else for my situation and started telling my interviewer how it was—that the mistakes I had made were my own and I had cleaned up my life. I kept my cool. The man was just asking questions and doing his job, I told myself. I explained everything I had done, all the legal problems in my past. All of that took about half an hour and I asked him when I would find out if I was accepted. He said, "We don't know. You'll get a letter in the mail."

Now I was waiting again with no clear idea when I would hear back. After another few months, I got the letter saying I was accepted, and letting me know the citizenship ceremony would be in Minneapolis on May 26, 2015. Amy, the two boys, and I went to Minneapolis. I Vlogged the whole event. There were many different races and countries represented at the ceremony. Knowing the English language is not a requirement for citizenship and we heard many different languages. Afterward, I said, "Okay—now I'm a citizen." I didn't feel any different, but I was feeling good knowing I could get on with my life.

In the end, I was glad Trump shook things up with immigration and, in a way, forced me to become a citizen. If anyone else had been in office I never would have gone through the effort. I would have stayed comfortable and not put myself through those months of waiting. The process made me realize I can do and be what I want here in America. There are laws I have to follow. When I was younger, I hated authority, rules, or anyone telling me what to do. There are still things I do not understand or like, but they are a part of the U.S. Government and I follow the rules and pay my taxes.

My message to immigrants is this: There are opportunities everywhere here in America. If you follow the rules there is nobody to stop anyone from doing what they want to do and creating the life they want in this country. The only person to stop us from achieving what we want in life is ourselves. Growing up, I always blamed other people. I blamed not having the right dad, being poor, not having this, or that. When I stopped playing that blame game and saw it was all up to me, I started to realize a path to create the life I want. This is America and everyone can create their own hustle.

14

CONSTANTLY IMPROVING

Becoming a rap star was my hidden fantasy for many years. I wanted to entertain and be someone who could engage an audience. I'm sure my shyness played into this fantasy. When you grow up not knowing how to talk to or communicate with people, secretly you imagine yourself overcoming these limitations. I pictured myself appearing in front of thousands of people, without having the first idea of how to make that happen. There were so many areas where I needed to improve if my dreams were going to become reality. My vision was one of traveling and speaking. I had a really great story to tell and I wanted to be good at telling it.

After discovering a group called Toastmasters, which trains people to become better public speakers, I found myself driving to meetings an hour and a half away in Mankato every week for about six months. This was early on in my quest for self-improvement. Toastmasters was more than just a time of training for learning how to speak and communicate. This was a wonderful experience of connecting with a wide variety of different people. I learned this was called "networking" and completely enjoyed connecting with people and making new friends. Networking was a powerful tool! The connection and power of networking are key to finding and having the right people to help you get to where you want to be in life and in business.

Now I sincerely believe God puts people in your life for a reason and those people are a gift to you that you need to recognize. Ever since I got sober and clean, I have had many people appear in my life just when I needed them. That is why I take the opportunity today to get to know and network with people.

My first Toastmasters speech was called an icebreaker and, while I was nervous, it went quickly. Come to think of it, I had become used to sharing the details of my life at my 12-step meetings, at the treatment center, and during my talks for the prison inmates. What I shared in those settings was very authentic, raw, and uncut. Anxious to improve my delivery. Toastmasters provided a platform for me to step up my speaking skills, though much improvement is still needed as I continue to strive to be a better communicator.

While I no longer picture myself as a glamorous rapper on the big stage, I have had the opportunity to participate on a live panel with eight other people speaking at the Green Industry Expo. Recently I had the honor of being one of the speakers at a Jobber Professional Development Day. My topic was Balancing Work, Family, and Mental Health. Heavy stuff for a kid who never believed in himself. I am grateful for the mentors in my life who believed in me even more than I did in myself. For a long time, I didn't understand that taking care of myself came before I could help or care for anyone else.

Every time I take steps to improve or learn something new, it makes me a better person and gets me closer to becoming the person I desire to be. I can honestly say that today I network with as many people as possible. Whatever I want to learn or do, I find people who can help me and get connected. I pay to learn or barter some of my knowledge and skill for theirs. Money spent on knowledge is never wasted—it pays back.

15

RESTRUCTURING THE BUSINESS AND FAMILY PRIORITIES

When the Covid-19 pandemic hit in March of 2020, both our landscaping and embroidery businesses were shut down for two weeks. I was terrified the shut-downs would last longer than that and I knew we were unprepared to deal with the economic consequences. I made the quick decision to lay off my employees and ride out the pandemic on what we had in savings. Would I have to declare bankruptcy and start all over or would we be able to ride this out?

We made it through the shutdown and upon reopening, I had a whole new outlook on how we would run the business in a way that would make us more financially stable and have more cash in reserve. Simply put, we scaled back. I had to decide where I was going to grow and what department needed to be dropped. We ended up scaling back the landscaping business and ramping up the embroidery side. We hired back everybody in the embroidery shop and lost two landscaping employees.

It was frightening to think that everything we had sacrificed for could be gone. No one knew what the future held and the situation was out of our control. The only thing we can control is how we prepare for anything like this that might happen again. There will be no excuses on my end.

I traveled to Georgia to speak with my good friend, Eric Benton, and take some time to decompress from the pandemic worries. He is also in the lawn care business. I consulted with him to get his ideas of how to weather this unexpected storm we were going through. After speaking with him I came home and restructured.

The company was shut down completely for two weeks and even after that restrictions were still in place for many businesses. Everyone still had to have their grass mowed. Fortunately, we had been designated as an essential business. That part of the business came back, but there was still uncertainty, and people were not prepared to spend a lot on landscaping and hardscaping. We lost hundreds of thousands of dollars on projects that were cancelled at the beginning of the season. Eventually, people staying home wanted to beautify their backyard and business began to ramp back up.

Our embroidery business took a huge hit. There were no sports, trade shows, or meetings, and not much need for customized business apparel. We had to get creative with different marketing and products. When masks became mandatory, we jumped on mask production, figuring out how to make masks on our machines. Our vendors started carrying them. We followed the demand and began to sell more masks than shirts.

During my trip to see Eric in Georgia, I acquired an unexpected addition to our family. Eric and his wife Krissie have three dogs. One of them is a huge Great Pyrenees named Hank. I was afraid of that dog as soon as I walked into their house. Hank weighs 150 pounds and was coming right at me to greet me at the door. The longer I stayed at the house, the more I fell in love with him. He was so calm and quiet and I fell in love with his personality. Hank would come over to me and put his face in my lap. He couldn't move very fast because of his size. By the end of my stay with Eric, I asked him if he could find me a dog like Hank. Eric's wife, Krissie, sent Amy a picture of their dog and Amy thought the dog was cute. Then she sent Amy a picture of a Great Pyrenees puppy. Of course, what is cuter than a fluffy, white puppy? Krissie texted Amy saying, "Chant is bringing home a puppy." Amy's response was, "Yeah, right. He'll never bring home a dog." At the time, Krissie didn't know I was actually planning on bringing one home.

Before I met Hank the Great Pyrenees, I never had any interest in having a dog. I thought about my kids and how they always wanted a dog. I was the dad who always said "NO—what do we need that for?" While I was down in Georgia, I thought a lot about what was happening in the country and the world. Life is too short to deny my kids the simple joy of having a pet. Eric found a breeder with puppies for sale, and I brought home an 8-week-old puppy we called Georgie.

When I was ready to leave Georgia for the 1500- mile trip back to Minnesota, Georgie was going with me. I knew nothing about dogs. We left late in the afternoon, around 5 or so. I stopped to take the dog out every two hours or so to give him food, water, and a rest stop. He and I bonded on that trip.

Amy was surprised; the boys were delighted! Georgie was small at that time, but he is not small anymore and we all love him. Georgie loves Minnesota. No better place for a big long-haired dog to play in the snow!

I was home without working for two weeks. The only thing I had to do was to spend that time with the family. We got some projects done around the house and worked together. The experience of 2020 made me realize how important family is no matter what is happening with the business. Now I have restructured my work schedule to have a lifestyle to include my family. If the pandemic had never happened, I would still be going, going, going. I still do plenty of that but now make sure I'm at home more.

16

PASSING IT ON TO THE NEXT GENERATION

The Hustle concept for me is to do what it takes to have the type of life that I did not have growing up. The Hustle is going out there and getting it. There are opportunities everywhere in America, I just had to learn how to recognize them. When I started, before we had kids, I worked seven days a week. I did that for several years trying to have what I never had, trying to pay off debt, and take care of our everyday bills. The Hustle is getting out there and working!

My biggest challenge now is continuing to grow as an individual and in business. It is easy to get complacent when things are going well, but I never want to feel like I have it all figured out. That is what I deal with today. Complacency is the enemy—the opposite of The Hustle.

In the beginning, I loved getting into the dirt and digging, getting my hands dirty. I grew that landscaping business but I got bored and wanted to move on to something else. First lawn and landscaping, then snow removal. My hands have been in a lot of businesses and I enjoy the process of building them and seeing where each one might take me. The embroidery operation right now is my love. I am enjoying it because I am growing it bigger and realizing its potential.

My goals and dreams are not material. I sometimes post what I would like to have, but it doesn't make sense to me to have that expensive car or house right now. Those things are nice to have, but they don't produce income and security. I posted a picture of a beautiful house on *Facebook*. Amy would love to have that home. If I get to the point where I could build that dream house, I would do it for her. We still live in our 700-square-foot house and we are building the business so we can afford those things if we want them. Money provides choices you do not have without it. Struggling to meet expenses every day is no way to live. We are content in knowing we have enough to get out of a bad situation if necessary.

Our little company sponsors kids' sports in our town. I have been active in a leadership program for the community. That group invests in entrepreneurs who show leadership potential. There are many great people in this small town of 3,200. Downtown is not flourishing as much as it was before. There are more services than retail outlets. The community is very tight—everybody knows everybody in this historic town. Downtown we have a small coffee shop, chiropractor, hair salon, insurance office, and an auto parts store.

While we love our community, we have never relied on that support to help our business. At the start of our embroidery operation, I felt the community was still upset with us for closing the only laundromat in town to start something else. Even though we employ local people, I heard whispers of, "All he cares about is money and starting an embroidery shop." Only ten percent of our business in the shop is from local sources and ninety percent online from around the world. We can't force anybody to spend money in our shop but we provide the best service for our neighbors if they choose to shop here. I hope they see how the business is flourishing because of the way we do things. We want to make them go, "Wow—this is a great company to have in our town."

After two years in operation, we employ six full-time people in the embroidery shop. Winter is part-time in the plowing operation, also with six employees. During the summer we have three on the team. When we started we could hardly support ourselves and now we have an obligation to all our valued employees, making sure we have work for them. They get paid before Amy and I get paid.

There are about five other landscapers in Jackson. My operation also serves several other towns. Spirit Lake, Iowa is just south of us and those clients are on the lake—a good source of business. I get along with most of the other businesses in town. Some of them feel intimidated, it seems, by our success. While I started with only a truck and a shovel, now we bid jobs and sometimes their customers choose us.

My biggest challenge today is finding that work/life balance for Amy and our boys. I feel I'm getting better at this. I grew up with the idea that I had no dad, so I never want Ashton and Cole to feel that way. That is why I am building a team. I am "buying" my time back by hiring people to do some of the things I used to do myself so I can be there for my family. What is all this work worth if my boys grow up and don't remember their dad being in their life.

When you grow up without a father, not even knowing who he was, you get used to people giving up on you. That has taught me how important it is to be a father and to take care of my family. It has taught me to never make any excuses as to why my life isn't what I imagined. I have made my plan for my life and the only reason why it might change is if God has a different plan for me.

Strangers and mentors became my role models and father figures until I found myself and what my purpose in life is. For the first nine years of Ashton's life—he is now eleven—I was constantly working. Now I make it to his games and we are starting to work together. *Ashton's Firewood* is a business he and I started last year. We get wood and split it, letting it dry for a year. We have found a supplier that already has dry wood for us to split up. We bundle it and deliver it or people come by the shop to pick it up outside. It's on the honor system. They can leave payment in the box outside or pay online. Ashton is excited about that. When there are nice days and he's not in school we'll go down and split the wood together and bundle it up. We have inventory in the spring for the camping season and in winter for indoor fireplaces.

Back when we had the laundromat Ashton's business was the soda machine in the building. Every summer he'd open it up and run it until fall. He'd fill up the machine and collect the money every two weeks. I get a kick out of my budding entrepreneur. It's important that I teach my sons how to work and learn some of the skills they will need in this world. I want both my boys to know they have a father who will be there to guide them. I understand how it feels to grow up without that feeling. Lost and confused as I was, I have come to a place in life where I have accepted my past and it has made me a better father.

I have a good relationship with my brothers and sisters. My mom lives close by and I keep in touch with her, but she is an independent lady and does her own thing—always out and about enjoying her life. Not your typical grandma. I have never met my oldest sister in person. She lives in Laos, has a husband and children. I am in touch with her on Facetime. Amy's parents are the opposite—the doting grandparents—and the boys love going over to their house.

Today my vision and goal are clear. There is no time for negativity, nor will I put up with anything that doesn't align with how I want to feel or who I want to be. I've been told all my life I wouldn't do or be anything great. I heard that from even the closest people around me. I am okay with that. It is in the past. I know now I can always find a solution to my problem because I know the only person who won't give up on me is me.

I am grateful for my wife, Amy, for being such an amazing wife and mother. There is nothing we have gone through together that we have not been able to work out. I am grateful for our two boys who I know will grow up to be productive, good citizens and add something positive to this world. I love the community of Jackson that Amy and I call our home. I am grateful for the opportunities and new friends we have met. The world is full of great people and I love connecting with them. I want to learn and experience new things as much as possible.

I told Amy years ago I wanted to write a book someday. This is one of the hardest things I have ever done and the book will be around even when I am no longer here. I am grateful to all of you who have been following my journey. You can't take the Hustle out of the kid who never had anything! The fire is lit and it can't be put out. Keep the Hustle alive and do your best. Remember—if you fall, always fall forward, never backward.

Made in the USA
Columbia, SC
19 November 2021